MARCEL GRANDJANY

music for the harp

collected transcriptions:

Pavane et Bransles	Anthoine Francisque
Aria and Rigaudon	Gottfried Kirchoff
Prelude and Toccata	George Frideric Handel
Saraband	George Frideric Handel
The King's Hunt	John Bull

ISBN 978-0-7935-7179-6

Associated Music Publishers, Inc.

DISTRIBUTED BY

HAL•LEONARD®
CORPORATION

7777 W. BLUEMOUND RD. P.O. BOX 13819 MILWAUKEE, WI 53213

c o n t e n t s

EXPLANATION OF SIGNS

 To connect only the next note.

 To prepare, or replace a group of 3 or 4 fingers playing in the same direction, ascending or descending.

✦ To muffle (strings previously played).

✦✦ To muffle the lower register (Wire strings). When this sign is placed between the two staffs, it indicates that all strings are to be muffled with both hands.

✦✦ or ✦✦. Indicates to muffle completely the lower register with the left hand in two motions, either ascending or descending.

✦......... Indicates series of quick muffled sounds either Right hand or Left hand.

+ Always indicates the THUMB OF THE LEFT HAND playing in the usual position of muffled sounds, but observing carefully the NOTE-VALUES.

Also indicates to stop the vibrations of strings previously played. THE NOTE PLAYED BY THE THUMB SHOULD NOT BE MUFFLED.

④ Indicates that the 4th finger of the Left hand must play in the usual position of muffled sounds, stopping the vibrations of strings previously played, observing the NOTE-VALUES.

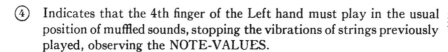

THIS POSITION OF MUFFLED SOUNDS, OBSERVING THE NOTE-VALUES, MUST BE CONSTANTLY USED WHEN PLAYING OCTAVES IN THE LOWER REGISTER (WIRE STRINGS) BY STEP-WISE PROGRESSION, ASCENDING OR DESCENDING.

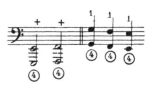

 Muffle the indicated notes by replacing the finger on the string without playing.

L.V. Let vibrate.

, To leave, quickly, after the note without muffling.

✳——— Series of notes "detached" (not muffled) (Always quick "lifted hand" wrist motion).

❜ To leave after the note to "SUSTAIN" the tone. (Slow "lifted hand" or "dropped hand", wrist motion.

〰〰〰 Play on the lower part of strings.

〰〰〰 Play close to the sounding board.

Marcel Grandjany

music for the harp

Pavane et Bransles
from "Le Trésor d'Orphée"

Free transcription for Harp by
Marcel Grandjany

Anthoine Francisque
1570-1605
French school of the Lute

Pavane

(1) For the lower B, tune and play lower C♭

Bransles

Vivace, molto Ritmico ($\text{♩} = 108$)

First Bransle of Montirandé

Risoluto

Second Bransle of Montirandé

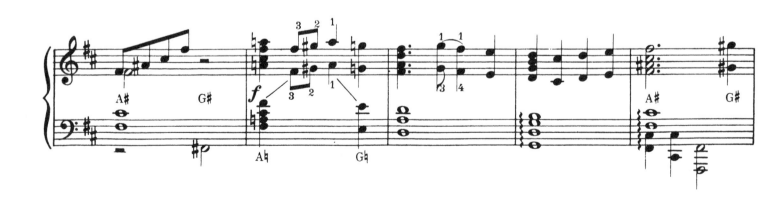

Aria and Rigaudon

Harp adaptation by
Marcel Grandjany

Gottfried Kirchhoff
(1685-1746)

Aria

2nd time: *pp, dolce, a little lower on strings*

*Play the lower C, immediately after the chord

Rigaudon

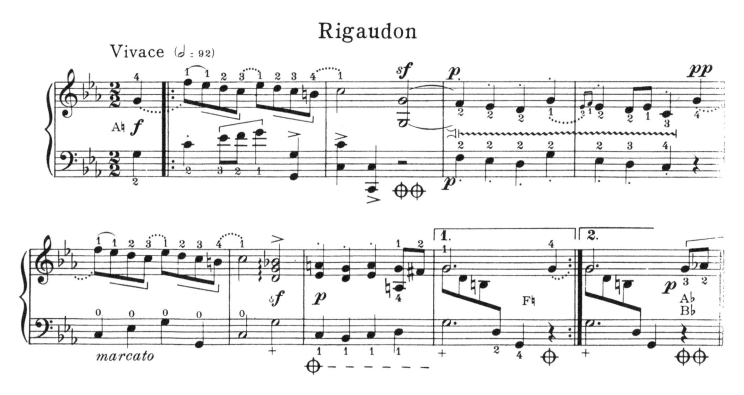

Prelude and Toccata

Free transcription for Harp
"Arpeggiando" ad libitum
written by Marcel Grandjany

Handel

Prelude

Harp

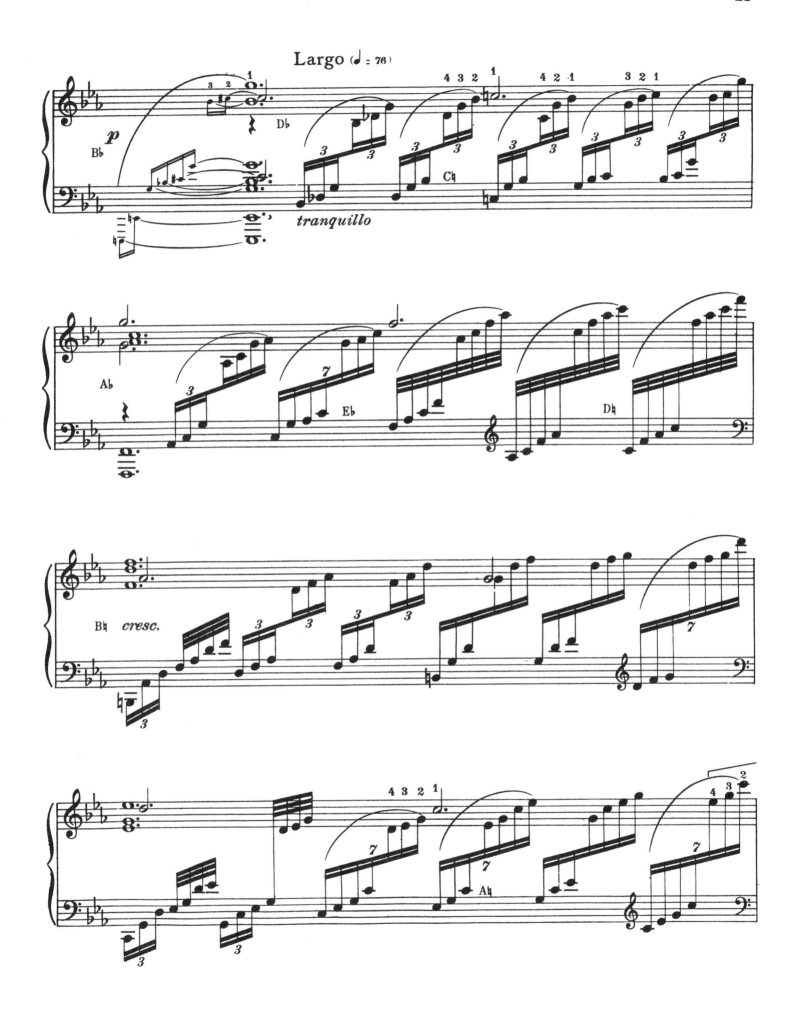

Toccata in C minor

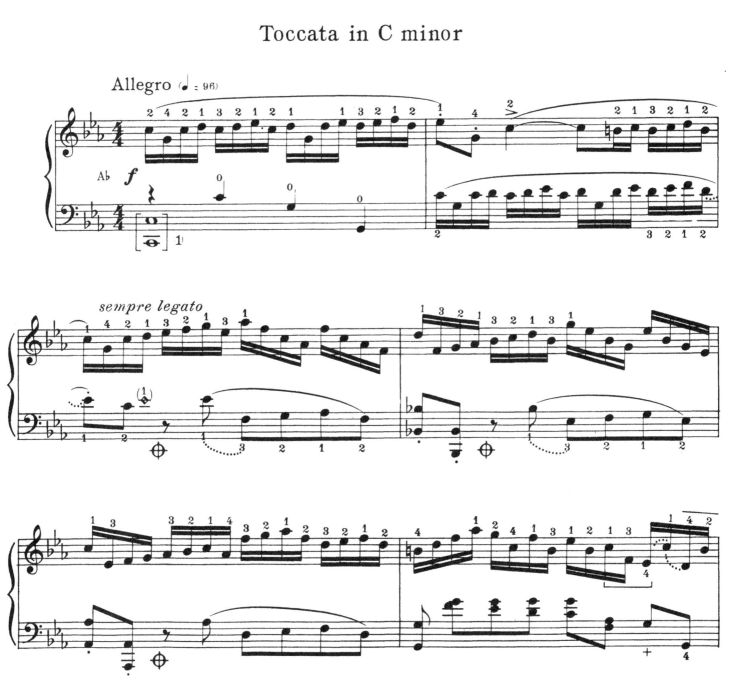

(1) When the Toccata is played immediately after the Prelude, omit the C Bass on the first beat.

Saraband

Harp adaptation by
Marcel Grandjany

Handel

N.B. The chord on the second beat, "unbroken" and softer than the first.

The King's Hunt

Harp adaptation by
Marcel Grandjany

John Bull 1563 - 1628
From the Fitzwilliam Virginal Book

Harp

also, lower on strings

staccato

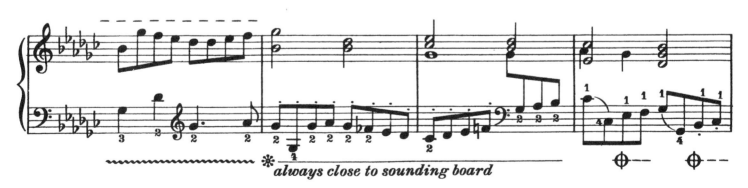

❋ *always close to sounding board*

The King's Hunt-6

④